Trying
Again
to
Stop
Time

Trying
Again
to
Stop
Time

SELECTED POEMS

JALAL BARZANJI

Sabah A. Salih, *Translator*

 The University of Alberta Press

Published by

The University of Alberta Press
Ring House 2
Edmonton, Alberta, Canada T6G 2E1
www.uap.ualberta.ca

LIBRARY AND ARCHIVES CANADA
CATALOGUING IN PUBLICATION

Barzanji, Jalal
[Poems. Selections. English]
    Trying again to stop time : selected
poems / Jalal Barzanji ; Sabah
A. Salih, translator.

(Robert Kroetsch series)
Issued in print and electronic formats.
ISBN 978-1-77212-043-1 (pbk.).—
ISBN 978-1-77212-074-5 (pdf).—
ISBN 978-1-77212-072-1 (epub).—
ISBN 978-1-77212-073-8 (kindle)

    I. Salih, Sabah A., translator. II. Title.
III. Series: Robert Kroetsch series

PS8603.A788A28 2015   C891.5971
C2014-908276-2
C2014-908277-0

First edition, first printing, 2015.
Printed and bound in Canada by Houghton
Boston Printers, Saskatoon, Saskatchewan.
Copyediting and proofreading by
Peter Midgley.

A volume in the Robert Kroetsch Series.

The University of Alberta Press is committed
to protecting our natural environment.
As part of our efforts, this book is printed
on Enviro Paper: it contains 100% post-
consumer recycled fibres and is acid- and
chlorine-free.

The University of Alberta Press gratefully
acknowledges the support received for
its publishing program from The Canada
Council for the Arts. The University of
Alberta Press also gratefully acknowledges
the financial support of the Government
of Canada through the Canada Book Fund
(CBF) and the Government of Alberta
through the Alberta Media Fund (AMF) for
its publishing activities.

Contents

IN 1976, Jalal Barzanji had just begun his teaching career at a primary school in the tiny mountainous village of Sktan, some seventy miles from Kurdistan's regional capital of Erbil (or what the locals call Hawler), when he unexpectedly found himself in love. Allowing their daughter marry a teacher would not be a problem, said the girl's family to Barzanji, but letting her marry a teacher-poet was out of the question. That's how the culture was, and still is. Even with jobs, poets are generally seen to be incapable of raising a family.

The little crisis of his love for the girl passed, but a bigger crisis, namely, what it meant to be a poet, had just begun. The isolation of village life made Barzanji look inward, deep into himself and his world. The questions were many and always complicated, the answers were seldom satisfying, and the rewards, though often meagre, required hours and hours of thinking and rethinking. And then there was this constant state of anxiety—anxiety about words and ideas, about culture and society, about politics and the government—that never seemed to go away. Though the three years in Sktan were a hard on a young man unused to the absence of running water, electricity and other modern conveniences, the experience, as he himself often acknowledges, did help anchor Barzanji's poetry in themes and concerns that continue to define his craft to this day: meditations on nature, reflections on the complexities of human emotions and situations, the way language and culture both collide and co-operate, what poetry can and cannot do, and the villagers' way with words—features not hard to detect even in his first published poems.

Appropriately titled *The Evening Snow Dance*, this first work also helps situate Barzanji in the multi-layered narrative of what could be described as Modern Kurdish poetry. Barzanji belongs to a generation of Kurdish poets, writers, and political campaigners from Iraqi Kurdistan (or Southern Kurdistan) who came of age in the late 1970s. This was the heyday of Socialist Realism. Art and literature were supposed to be easily accessible to the general public; more important, they were supposed to play an important role in the Kurdish people's long struggle against Saddam Hussein, whose basic plan for Kurdistan was to Arabize it by force. The Iraqi regime's overwhelming embrace of Socialist Realism meant that Modern Kurdish poetry tended to take a decidedly pro-Soviet and anti-American line.

While he, too, was politically sympathetic to Moscow's line, Barzanji could not, aesthetically, allow himself to be drawn to a view of literature that paid lip service to artistic freedom and creativity. For him, mixing literature and politics just didn't seem to be the right thing to do. This point looms rather large throughout his poetry. Militancy, certainty, political urgency, ideological purity—these are largely absent from his poetry. More than anything else, one encounters ambiguity, symbolism, imagism, curiosity about language, and, since coming to Canada in 1998, the losses and gains that come with a hybrid identity.

If this sounds like a partial description of a poet who has come under the spell of Western Modernism, it is. Though he is well versed in classical Kurdish poetry, and though he continues to return to its masters (Wafaie, Haji Qadiri Koyee, and Mahwe in particular), Barzanji seems to have decided, and in my judgement rightly so, that such models are there for inspiration only, not for emulation. As a poet made cosmopolitan and out-of-place by globalization, he had to seek his models elsewhere. It is, therefore, perfectly understandable for Barzanji to have formed an attachment to Western Modernism, in particular to its pioneers, most notably Charles Baudelaire and T.S. Eliot, so early in his career. Modernism, by emphasizing experimentation in technique and writing style, by insisting that the artist should be accountable to no one but art, by being suspicious of mass politics, and by welcoming cultural and linguistic mixing in art, has offered a more attractive alternative to traditional and local views of art, which in general tend to subject art to political, religious, and moral controls. The result is that in Barzanji's case one doesn't have to be either Kurdish or knowledgeable about Kurdish culture and history to feel a connection to his poetry.

As Barzanji himself has said in conversation, to be a poet in the modern world is to feel like an outsider everywhere. It is a world in which cultural borders are fast disappearing and, as a consequence, the poet can no longer be satisfied with just addressing a local audience or just trying to modernize a native tradition. It is a world in which Western Modernism continues to be a big player in shaping not just artistic and literary creations but also architecture and styles of living. In that respect Barzanji's poetry is shaped by pressures and challenges not all that different from those shaping the poetry of so many other contemporary poets—Taslima Nasrin, Adonis, Yehuda Amichai, Shuntaro Tanikawa easily come to mind. Like theirs, Barzanji's is a voice in which the native willingly mutates into the global.

This translation follows the order of the original Kurdish text, *Trying Again to Stop Time and Other Poems* (published by Aras Press in Erbil, Kurdistan, in 2009), a reprint in one volume of Barzanji's previously published collections: *Trying Again to Stop Time* (2009), *I Want to Be Named Home* (2007), *In Memory of a Person Swept By the Wind* (2006), *The Rain of Compassion* (2002), *No Warmth* (1985), and *The Evening Snow Dance* (1979). There are three more recent poems at the end, which appear for the first time in print in this translation.

SABAH A. SALIH
Professor of English
Bloomsburg University, Pennsylvania, 2014

I CAN MAKE NO ASSUMPTION on the part of readers, nor give them any specific ideas about my poems before they have actually read them. I would like readers to form their own connection to these poems and to shape their own opinions on them. I have published several books of poetry, but I have never introduced any of them. However, this time I am publishing for different readers, many of whom are not familiar with Kurdish poetry. I don't know who first said "All Kurdish people are poets," but I have always considered this adage be true, because most Kurdish writers began by writing poetry, me included. I didn't attend any creative writing courses, yet the reading of literature slowly turned into a love for writing for me. I took a special interest in poetry. I began with love poetry, but this did not fulfil my initial ambitions of attracting women, so I expanded my notions of love to include beauty, human desire, nature, and peace. These have become the only way I can exist this world, and bring back the things I have lost in life. I also created images from my words and thoughts of beauty. When I started writing poetry in 1970 there was no university in Kurdistan, no newspapers or literary magazines; nor were there resources I could draw on, except for a small library in Hawler that housed a few hundred Kurdish books. The rest were all in Arabic, since the Iraqi regime did not allow Kurdish people to receive an education in their mother tongue. My education was therefore in Arabic, which gradually became my second language. In the library I read some books about Kurdish, Arabic and Western literature. I was influenced by Western poets like Baudelaire, Rimbaud, Saint-John Perse, and T.S. Eliot, among others.

In 1970 most Middle Eastern countries demanded Socialist Realism from their writers. I couldn't agree with this, because I wanted to write without interference, to give expression to what was inside me without any ideology or political grandstanding to inhibit my imagination. On the other hand, there was a demand for resistance poetry that supported the struggle of the Kurdish people for freedom. Then again, there was heavy censorship aimed at keeping the media and everything revolving around it state-run. Writers were never given accolades for their work; instead they were jailed, tortured, killed, and persecuted in different ways. I decided, however, to write beyond the rules, and to create an empty canvas for readers, allowing them to use their own minds to paint on it. The dictatorship didn't want to allow readers such unlimited access to my voice. I knew I had to stand up for the rights of Kurdish people, but I didn't write any resistance poems to encourage people to go to war because I think that overt protest poetry takes writers way from aesthetics, which is what interests me. Besides, I wanted to write for the world, not just for Kurds. I kept to the aesthetics of my poetry, but I wrote columns about peace, cultural cleansing, and social justice. Thus I worked through words for liberation, and these efforts were enough of a crime for the Iraqi regime. I paid a heavy price for my writing—this story appears in my memoir, *The Man in Blue Pajamas*, published by the University of Alberta Press.

Poems use words as weapons, and words don't have the power to change regimes. Yet dictatorships fear bold writers who speak out against them. They censor writers heavily, making them write under conditions of fear, hoping that they will hide something and constrain their minds. I used symbolism and masks to express myself. Sometimes using these tools will take you way from your real feelings, and may this affect your writing in many ways.

I published my first book of poetry in 1979 under the title *The Evening Snow Dance*. It was well received by Kurdish readers as a new work written in a modern style, and with timely vision. Crossing borders, and being away from my birthplace, along with the experience of exile, becoming involved with a broader writing community of writers in Canada and having freedom of expression, has brought new materials, new vision and new landscapes into my poetry. Some of these poems appear in this collection and I encourage readers to find their own interpretations in them.

JALAL BARZANJI

Edmonton, November 2014

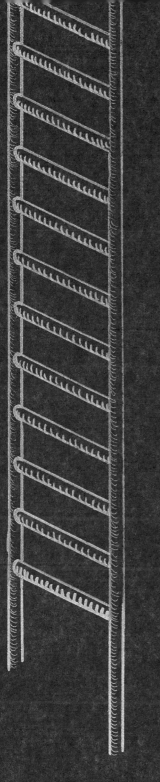

Trying
Again
to
Stop
Time

2009

Trying Again to Stop Time

At sunrise
time begins to depart;
at sundown
time turns into intense darkness.

When I travel,
I can't wait to arrive,
but when I arrive,
I see that time is there already.

Sometimes,
no more than a quick look toward the east is needed
for my past to turn into present;
in a flash time takes me back to reality—
it resembles a wooden stretcher,
like the one leaning against a mosque wall.

With the hours of love coming to an end,
time becomes my biggest obstacle,
even as my wife and I reach ecstasy.

It's a losing battle:
my words have no chance against time.
Sometimes,
unable to catch up with imagination,
I leave the battle, candle in hand,
in complete darkness.

Sometimes,
nature, too, is like that:
grass is unstoppable in the spring,
but in autumn it is in full retreat.

Often I see my words sinking in time's depth.
Often I see some of these words resurfacing,
the little waves they create fleeing away sheepishly.
It's a battle I can never win.

1

The middle stream
pours into a different life;
you have yet to experience it,
but it's no stranger to you.

2

Since childhood,
my imagination had been pulling me to the north,
into the heart of winter.
Once there,
it abandoned me
for good.

3

One morning,
long ago,
juice from an apple
dripped onto my words,
leaving them stained forever.

4

Ever since imagination has become my guide,
it's been trying to conquer shame
in the hope of going everywhere naked.

...

7

Don't throw stones:
sunshine is all around you—
you may hit its soul.

8

At the burial site of his legs,

the youth turned to God:

"God, how can I manage without legs?

You could surely have given my legs a second chance,

let them grow like grass.

You could surely have rendered the mine harmless.

You knew Saddam Hussein

had planted it in the meadow

near our house,

but you let it go off

while I was studying!"

9

Every evening in exile,

I try to paint the clouds,

but I always fail:

they're way too fast for my brush.

10

My wife,

on my fifty-fifth birthday,

gave me a walking stick

from a tree

known not for strength but weakness.

11

Look what they're doing to me:

they say they have no time,

they're too exhausted.

Yet somehow they always find the time and energy

to be cruel to me.

We drove to the sea,
so that water and earth
could reunite us with the sky.

On the way,
even the mountains
and sunset
had been taken over by trees;
animals were too eager to welcome visitors.

Vendors along the roadside
sold strawberries;
they were no different
from those selling grapes and pomegranates
between Hawler and Suleimaniya.

At the campground,
we pitched a tent,
built a fire,
grilled chicken.
Fear of bears coming down from the mountains
kept me awake all night.
My mother had taught me
to always be afraid of animals.
I know a mouse is nothing,
but the smallest creature makes me run.

In the morning mist,
we brought our fire back to life:
coffee, fried eggs, and toast.
It tasted so good.

As we got on the road again,
my wife said:
"Twenty five years, and you still can't drive."
"This time around it's not my fault," I protested,
"it's the view."

The next day,
by early morning,
we were in Vancouver.
The rugged mountains looked intimidating,
but the city seemed to have a soft heart:
with freshness and colour,
it welcomed all visitors.

1
The freedoms I have tasted in dreams
I haven't tasted anywhere else—
not even in writing.

...

3
Writing
has given me a pencil as tall as me,
so that I can colour the world.

4
Please don't shoot
when I am dreaming.

...

13
I know
after my death
time will enjoy turning my soul
into a straw hat.

14
My first major crisis happened
at home—
exile was its cause.

15
My feeling is
the grassland
where my poetry grazes.

16
Knowledge,
accompanied by thinking,
paid ignorance a visit.

17
The mark left by your little smile
is still there.

18
Slowly,
I approach death's beautiful waterfall.

19
The bowl
of my life,
full of sorrow,
I leave behind.

...

22
When you are here,
life is different.

...

25
Fear
won't allow me to be free.

26
I saw beauty
running after the colours of a butterfly.

27
The moon
above the battlefield
is sad.

28
My imagination has lost its way—
too late to do anything about it.

...

33
Music became my horse.
I went hunting for the soul.

34
The apple
that has fallen from heaven
has landed in a woman.

Friend,
let us return to the time before displacement,
when the two of us,
schoolbooks in hand,
went to Kooran Park on Fridays
to study for our exams.
I wonder what became of this park:
has it too been devoured?
You became an agricultural engineer and a poet,
got a job at Kalachi Yaseen Agha,
taking care of trees
the way you took care of your sisters.
You said the pomegranates were your favourite.
You also said there was nothing more magical
than hearing prunes fall at night.
For my part, I became a teacher and poet.
My first job took me to the village of Sktan,
where I wrote my first collection of poems,
The Evening Snow Dance.
It was there also where
one autumn
I became friends with trees.

Friend,
I still remember
the two of us studying by street lights;
one time I showed you my art work,
the sun half hidden by a mountain.
I wish the two of us could go back to the Hawler of the 1980s:
Remember our walks during summer nights?
Remember all the poems we recited?
Remember how unafraid we were,
even as the regime became more oppressive?

What about our evenings at the Civil Servants' Club?
We always sat under an old eucalyptus tree.
We liked to see the birds congregating on top.
We also liked the water fountain—
it taught us to appreciate silence.
And the friends we hung out with?
Some probably are dead;
others probably have become enemies.
You know how vicious politics can be.
In those days you could see the city's ancient citadel miles away.
Now urbanization has ruined the view;
it has also fragmented our childhood.

Friend,
There is no homecoming for me.
The roads I don't recognize;
time is also running out.
As you yourself said,
"No return for you."
My backache reminds me of that daily.
we are destined to die apart from one another.

Friend,
where I am now snow is constant—
a vast emptiness
stretching all the way to Alaska
is all I can see.
The cold turns everything blue.
Once the Gold Rush brought people here.
They came by train,
on horseback,
on foot.
Now there is only ruin and cold.

Friend,
I like your suggestion:
this time I am visiting.
We must go for a drive on Koya Road.
We must stop at one of the fields dotting the road
for those tiny sweet and sour cantaloupes
grown under the blazing sun,
amazingly,
without water.
I also want to see the city's old produce market—
maybe that too,
like the garden at the Civil Servants' Club,
is not there anymore.

Friend,
my mother used to bake her own bread
over an open fire;
she made yoghurt too.
Yes, my friend,
twelve years ago,
political oppression sent me to exile;
luck landed me in Canada.
I feel like I am trapped in the heart of winter forever.
I stare at the few crumpled papers from my prison days;
I don't know what to make of them.
Here in this house,
many great writers have come and gone,
but it is only the snow that remains ever present.
The other day,
I saw four men approaching
like shadows,
each resembling a season:
they all entered Jack London's cabin,

sat by the fireplace,
and before long
agreed on one thing:
winter meant grief.

Thanks to the sea,
the journey from Istanbul
to Edmonton
is a seventeen-hour flight.
A day earlier,
a thirteen-hour bus ride
brought us to Istanbul's Ataturk Airport.
It felt good to say goodbye to Sivas—
the city was too conservative for our taste.
The airport was teeming with refugees like us:
some sleeping,
some reflecting,
some stretching,
some looking up words
they thought they needed upon arrival in a foreign land,
some busying themselves with their hats,
some pondering the possibility of failure and disappointment,
some missing home,
some staring at their new lives in suitcases.

Some six months before,
we left Ankara for Sivas.
Nine months earlier,
in the midst of the Kurdish civil war,
I fled to Ankara,
where luck turned out to be on my side:
I was accepted by the UN as a refugee.
For six months
in the Ols district,
the hub of refugees from Southern Kurdistan,
I was Teža's tenant.
Every morning,
Sungul and I

climbed down 122 concrete steps
to go to the local bazaar:
Sungul sold ice water,
I reflected on what was to come.
I am not a storyteller,
though I do keep a lot in my heart.

In 1961,
at the start of the September Revolution,
Iraqi warplanes bombed our village.
For several weeks
the nearby caves were our home.
Mother missed her vegetable garden;
she knew it wouldn't survive under the rubble.
Father lost the few sheep he cared so much about.
And I lost a woollen ball I had made myself.

My first time flying
I was unafraid:
I had complete faith in my kite's wings.
The second time,
I flew from Ankara to Kiev
on a fake visa,
hoping to be smuggled to Sweden.
The venture failed;
I was caught
and sent back to Istanbul
on a half-empty flight.

My children weren't afraid of flying;
the plane going up and down was like a seesaw for them.
For my wife,
flying above the rain, the crowds, the city
was hard to believe.
In Amsterdam,
UN bags in hand,

we stood for six hours near the gate.

Getting lost was our biggest fear.

But I did manage to call Hawler.

I don't remember much else from Amsterdam.

Crossing the Atlantic

made me realize we were still without an address.

The Pocket

Sometimes,
it's a knife people pull out of their pockets
sometimes,
it's a flower
sometimes,
it's a cigarette
sometimes,
it's just a thread
sometimes,
it's a colouring pencil
sometimes,
it's a slingshot
sometimes,
it's just a small ball,
a watch,
a compass,
a flute,
a handkerchief,
a photo of a child,
a photo of a martyred father,
a mirror,
a Viagra pill,
a condom,
a small bottle of arak,
a pen (for signing a confession),
a cheat sheet,
bread and eggs,
sunflower seeds,
stolen fruit.
And sometimes this:
a malicious report against a friend.

Other times,

the pocket is used to protect the hand from the cold,

or to avoid a handshake,

or to avoid clapping,

or to hide tainted money,

or to cope with boredom,

or to imprison a little bird,

or to hide a wedding ring,

or to hide evidence of an affair,

or to hide a politician's self-incriminating letter,

or to hide stolen doves,

or to keep a mercy bullet.

Sometimes,

it's their second country's passport that people pull out,

some kissing it,

others just looking at it.

The stream and I
move together
in the dark,
in empty spaces,
in forests,
and in winter.
Together,
we bring nourishment to trees we don't even know;
then we move on.
When I fall behind,
the stream waits for me.
When the stream gets behind,
I wait for it.
Sometimes the stream is good company,
telling me great stories.
When the mist comes,
we change our clothes
and forget about time.
Amazingly,
we still don't know
how long we have been in each other's company.
Also,
I never thought it proper to ask
why the stream makes room for both the hunter and the hunted—
I know there may be some wisdom in this,
but I'm not sure.

The stream and I
move on.
Some mornings,
I turn to mist,
providing the stream with cover,
while it becomes my muse
as I stop,
trying to mimic the little waves.
We're like two travellers,
passing trains, old roads, and abandoned settlements.
As we continued our journey,
we learned that every village and town
had a different name for us.
At one point,
we saw a sailor
looking for wind.
We saw the moon too,
giving us,
though unwillingly,
its thick warm coat.
That night,
I had no need for rest;
I had no trouble getting up in the morning.
My poetry became inseparable from the waves and mountains.
In the end,
I didn't care in which direction the stream was heading,
but I was sure it was not heading to Koya.

Returning to Autumn

I'm not sure
you too can return to autumn,
but I must say
it's been a good return for me:
these past six days
I get good sleep,
I rise early,
I get to see the leaves fall,
and now that my words have turned into an orchard,
I don't need much.
I pick ripened fruit every morning
and thank autumn for helping me reconcile with myself.

I Want
To Be
Named
Home

2007

To Go Back and Back

1

I want the stream
that has been following me for years
to become my imitator.

2

The seagull left the sea,
flew far, far away,
but, unlike us,
it can return.

...

4

When I was a kid,
on my way to school,
I used to look at the grass
growing on both sides of the road.

...

6

When you return,
be sure to bring imagination along.

...

10

It's a good time
to fly for free.

11
Stop sending me letters
via the wind.

...

13
I'm still trying
to bridge the distance
between
my heart
and my new place.

14
When I return to my childhood,
I'll come straight to you.

...

16
Mine is the power of love;
theirs is the power of hate.

...

18
Under the soul,
freedom is all alone.

...

20
Next to a martyred son
a mother's footprint.

...

22
The colours
got lost between us.

...

25
Autumn
brings the world home.

26
The river
always gives us softer bodies.

27
In autumn
you were always a pleasant sunshine.

...

29
Loneliness
is driving the ocean
crazy.

30
The shade
we left behind by the river
is now a boat!

...

32
Even for burial,
he refused to change.

...

34
The road I took
on my return home
collapsed into the sea.

...

36
Tonight,
your story
bored me.

...

38
If you lose me,
you'll find me at a terminal.

39
The crowd
that used to steal my time
is still there.

...

41
I'm looking for a place
where I won't drown.

42
The trap
he laid
in his front yard
to catch a blackbird
collapsed
on his conscience.

...

44
An owl,
one autumn night,
was too frightened
of his own voice
to fall asleep.

...

46
I wouldn't like to be a king:
that would spoil my loneliness.

47
The fingers
that used to pray in the cold,
I see them no more.

...

49
My exile's roots
grow deeper by the day.

...

51
The children
drew the map of their homeland
on the dusty ground of their refugee camp.

52
The horizon
is where the day's peace and quiet ends.

...

55
The two of us,
in a poem,
become one.

57
A child
in Canada
was missing the mother tongue.

...

60
His third language
had no room for his memories.

61
My grandmother's stories
always failed to put me to sleep.

62
The war,
faster than lightning,
sent me to Canada.

64
My feeling,
faster than ink,
landed on paper.

65
The roads
do not take you to places;
they take you inside many hearts.

...

69
I continued staring at the stars
until my head became their home.

...

73
The sun has yet to ask the earth,
"How much do you owe me?"

...

76
Tonight,
the sweetness of the scenery
leads to ecstasy.

...

79
Doubt
didn't allow my prayer
to bring me certainty.

80

In the end,
what we give back to the earth
is the ultimate truth.

81

After the leaves are gone,
nature
zips up its trousers.

82

Wherever I am,
I feel out of place.
It's not my fault—
it's the wind's.

83

Art and childhood
always ask the same question:
"When are you coming back?"

84

The wind,
having robbed the earth of its cover,
settled in a valley.

...

87

I lost you while praying;
I haven't prayed since.

88
War
has made us refugees
in so many lands.

89
It was my memoir
that changed me.

...

93
Faster than a bird
flies my desire.

94
The shadow
and I
go for walks,
every evening,
together;
at night we share a bed.

...

96
Poetry
has taken me on many journeys—
always at night.

97
Exile
has helped my words create many a window.

98
To enter the mirror
we must all follow the same path.

99
Death
remains constant in all my dreams.

...

Beyond the Sky Is a Blue Window

Far, far away,

beyond the sky,

a blue window can be seen.

Someone

wearing a blue T-shirt

quickly comes to the window

and just as quickly disappears.

Nearby,

I see a blue wind

accompanied by a flock of birds—

all the trees welcome the birds

except a blue tree:

it likes neither the moon,

nor the birds.

Far, far away,

there is a blue mist;

there is also a woman wearing a blue dress.

On the highest rooftop,

a boy is flying a blue kite—

now I know what ails this one particular tree.

If God can hang his blue T-shirt

on a blue line,

so can you.

Now,

not very far from where I am,

I see a blue garden

where at any time you can visit with the birds.

Here,

the evening is blue;

the flowers reach the blue window.

It is very quiet here,

a great place to call home.

Maybe the person in the window
likes to come down
and go for a walk
every evening
wearing a blue T-shirt.
This is a garden
where you soon begin to smell like wheat,
where you soon find blue windows entering your heart.

A Woman Befriends Darkness

(Dedicated to a woman who lost her eyesight in the chemical attack on Halabja in 1988.)

The warplanes
robbed Halabja of wind.
The chemical attack
killed Omar Khawar
and the daffodils in his pocket.
The warplanes
poisoned drinking water
and ended the brief peace people had been enjoying.
The breeze
that carried pollen all the way to Sharazour
is no more.
The earth made sick in 1988
has been unable to leave its bed ever since.
Even now,
the teachers of Halabja have nightmares;
the pupils have forgotten how to play.
This particular woman has been blind since 1988:
ever since,
she has been unable to knit,
to milk her goat;
her sheep have been unable to walk.
For seventeen years now,
this woman has been unable to garden,
or to take a look at her daughter's face.
She can't even tell when the sun goes down by her tiny window,
or how grey her hair has become.
For seventeen years now,
darkness has been her sole companion,
for it is only darkness that she can see.

Between the two seas,
a woman was holding a stick,
trying to frighten dreams away.
A house martin was bringing water
to her chicks.
Between the two seas,
my patience,
badly bent,
had to rely on a walking stick—
the exile's gift.

Between the two seas,
my words are free,
but the sound of a peach falling
won't wake me up—
unless it falls into my hands.

Here,
poetry is free,
loneliness is free,
but here
the shepherd's sack
has no room for the sun.

Between the two seas,
a lantern was burning sadly,
while at the water's edge,
a fisherman was trying to regain hope,
as my imagination was trying to hide
behind my mother's bundle of clothes.

The woman continued
to chase dreams away.
There was plenty of snow,
even though it was sunny and warm
there was no one to be seen.

Here,
Everyone can express themselves freely,
but failure has only one father.
Here,
flowers have no smell.
Here,
freedom leads to boredom.
Here,
I have yet to see a horseman
in control of his animal.

Here,
I see no appreciation for black and white paintings.
Children show no interest in picking up abandoned eggs.
The beautiful,
who are always frightened,
are easy to hunt
and the clouds never stop looking for trouble.
I waited for this woman to arrive,
hoping that her fire
would put us back together again.

Thanks to globalization
the man drinks coffee in São Paulo
the night before he was in Tibet
on the way
he stopped in New Delhi
to buy incense
he lunched at a McDonald's
somewhere in Michigan
by evening
he was drinking a beer in Frankfurt
and now he's here
in Hawraman
eating walnuts under a walnut tree.

In Memory of
a Person
Swept
By the
Wind

2006

In Memory of a Person Swept By the Wind

In my memory,
plant a tree on every road you take.
In every city,
look for the nearest post office,
and send me a letter.

In my memory,
be gentle to the water you drink;
also, make sure that when the bodies of the dead
come home from exile,
they are properly sealed.

In my memory,
don't let the victims of recent genocide be forgotten,
always prefer Hawler's public library to its streets.
When you do go to our favourite teahouse,
remember to ask for an extra cup,
so that discussion can continue a bit longer.

That morning,
the sun refused to come into my room,
the wind refused to visit my garden.
I left my coffee unfinished,
my cigarette too.
"At least," I mused,
"My friend got my letter before he died."
Ice-water vendors were nowhere to be found.
Colours became indistinguishable from one another.
Words stopped coming.
I remained indifferent to my teeth,
to my mother's basil,
to my last dream.
That morning,
death was having the upper hand.

1

Death and I
went home,
sharing the same walking stick.
Dream followed us,
hoping to deceive us,
but we learned not to trust it.
Along the roadside,
kisses were growing wild,
but no pilgrims could be seen.
It was too late, anyway, for watching the sunset,
too late for the POWs' return,
too late to start fighting again,
too late even for mass suicide.
That is why now
I'm with the dogs,
with death,
with war,
with hunger,
and with the cold.

2

The guerrillas lost one more battle;
life is in retreat.
The moon came
but only for a very short time.
The butterflies have become good friends with death—
too late for watching the sunset.

1
There,
in a corner,
light and darkness
had been eager to meet.
For a while,
the sky seemed too narrow for flying;
what we experienced by day
seemed unfamiliar by night.
Little by little,
our memories were deserting us.
As exiles,
we didn't even dare to think of home.
There,
where the stars are,
life was returning home,
indifferent and morose.
There,
I left shame and sorrow behind.
That was a long time ago;
my father's water can flipped;
he never got another chance to water the flowers.
That was the time
when we buried the promises we made to God,
when we gave imagination a space of its own,
when we returned to Sktan by moonlight,
when we buried our martyrs.

2

One evening,

we were in Awagird,

the sun fixing its remaining rays on a martyr's grave.

Stuck in the desert were a group of wounded moons:

all women,

victims of Anfal.

The campaign turned the rain and the sky into strangers,

and the wind into an accomplice.

Spring too had turned its back on the victims.

God had lost control.

Non-intervention gave war the green light:

acting quickly,

it destroyed every dream the young had.

As we rushed to help,

bringing water from grandma's well,

we saw the moon

descending barefoot

and turning itself into a tent

for the children.

3

My father then was still living;

he had a talent for drawing.

He wasn't a city man;

he was a labourer without skills.

Every morning,

wearing a red cap,

he went looking for work.

The little money he made,

he spent on feeding his family.

One day,

he exchanged his cap for a blue one.

He had the blue cap on when he died.

4

Since 1988

all the apples die before they ripen,

the pomegranates shrivel in the dust.

That evening,

people in groups

were coming out of their cages,

but there was no water,

no horses.

The fortresses,

the masks,

the gigantic black rocks,

offered no protection.

5

I used to be able to understand dreams

and imagine a lot.

Now nature is too fast for me.

I have settled in a good-sized village,

but I can no longer carry my things to the rooftop.

I can, however, travel—

in a child's car—

and if my flowers are taken ill,

I can get help.

But here is not home:

the pear tastes so different;

doves do not gather near schools.

6

Last night,
I was getting ready for a trip
with two of my constant companions:
wind and luck.
My kite was up in the sky,
leaving the birds behind
and promising new beginnings.
But opening new windows is no longer for me.
Even the ladybugs didn't like to remain on my fingers;
they all flew away east,
towards my uncle's home.
I remember long ago
poetry coming to me
wearing a shirt made of water,
and sandals decorated with pearls,
asking me to make myself more visible.
I remember saying,
"No, I prefer a place where I can hide,
where I can sleep in peace and quiet,
where I can write poetry
without any control over my imagination."

1

Our conscience
has fallen asleep
on a chair.

2

The migrating birds spread their shadows above us,
but we only let them land in thorny fields.

3
There,
the rain always
reveals the sky's secrets.

4
The spiders
were building their webs
on half-ruined doors.

5
I have never allowed war,
otherwise known as growing up,
to spoil my childhood's water bowl.

...

8
After we let the wind be the custodian of our past,
we made friends with stones;
that's how we learned to be lazy.

9
The photos
in science books
stare at us—
blankly.

10
The birds
and
the hawks
changed the mood of the sky.

The
Rain
of
Compassion

2002

War

1

The war
ruined my morning,
threw my book into the sea,
and left me thinking about exile.

The war
forced me to end my evening game.
It left my imagination leafless
and landed me in the wilderness.

It even confused history.

2

The war
works like a lottery,
even though it is guided by ideology.

3

I have been behind locked doors
for a long, long time,
confused and irritated,
finding comfort
neither in hope nor in dreams.

4

It's one war after another.
I am still hoping for that day to come
when in the evening I can put my weapon away
and sleep all night without worry.

The women of my country
have become inseparable from the cemetery.
The keys were poisonous:
poison above,
poison below,
poison in the blood,
poison in the imagination.
We were small to begin with;
now we've become even smaller,
and more confused.

My country,
war has left you without gardens.
The young are jumping to their deaths.
The old are too old for walking sticks.
Your doors are always open,
but your windows are always shut.
There was a time when people grew wheat
built beautiful homes
went to the mountains
made music
organized festivals
and eliminated bad odours.

To exile,
we take with us
two eyes, one heart, and one soul.
When we return
we bring back thousands of eyes and thousands of hearts,
but we return with deeply troubled souls.
We plant trees in exile;
we socialize,
but only loneliness filters through our imagination.
Still, I must say hello to exile.

It was a divided nation:
too many wars,
too many tribes,
too many sects.
It was a divided land:
each day
losing a tree,
a spring,
a valley,
a cliff.
Neither its music,
nor its poetry
cared for dreams.

Life
took away
the lines
and the wings.
People returned from the flood,
only to fight again.
People returned from the desert at night,
the sword still at their side.
People returned from the mountains,
their memories of better times erased.
No one knew how to dance anymore.

Desire
is fighting with the woods
over what happened the night before.
In a room,
a tree is fighting with desire
over growth;
grass is in short supply.
For me, too,
the game is over.

The fallen doves
have been entangled in imagination
and imagination itself has been trapped by thorns.
Our history has fallen into a stream;
It is disappearing fast.
Only serenity can reignite desire.
The fallen doves
don't want to have anything to do
with a history that doesn't reside high up.

1

There was no shade anywhere;
the dream's body was the earth's pasture.
The earth,
by squeezing summer grass,
had managed to come up with a glass of water.
As for luck,
it had taken refuge among the reeds.
Desolation was becoming burdensome even for the clouds.
A poet was trying to follow an eagle,
the valley was in ruin,
the sea was in no hurry to fill up the jars.
Bad smells came from the bedrooms,
the wells,
the streams.
There were no walnuts on the trees,
no winds either.
It was the start of summer;
homes had their doors wide open;
grief was busy shortening lives.
Not too long ago,
there was plenty for the birds to eat;
women were good friends with the rain.
The fisherman,
the shepherd,
the woodsman,
the merchant had no reason to complain.
But now beauty was declaring,
"I have sealed my letter and have thrown it into a stream."
The shaman, however, remained hopeful:
"Clapping your hands makes all your wishes come true;
sleep for seven years, and you'll see the doves returning."

2

One of my legs is stuck in the west;

the other is trapped in the thick mud of the east.

All the milk is spilled;

the wind refuses to meet its obligations.

I stay away from the mirror,

but I see some people trying to rub sunshine on their hair,

while combing their desire in front of the mirror.

On the way home the other day,

I was thinking of my stolen keys,

and of why in the past

there was enough water even for the dead.

3

Greetings to you, tall grasses of the valleys.

We take our clothes off,

and mingle with you like music.

The crown is fallen;

the earth is fallen.

But the egg

from the other side of the world

can be seen.

If you don't already own a home, however,

you shouldn't be thinking about buying one now.

After seven years,

I'm returning to where the doves come to drink,

but I still cannot find my keys

and words are all I have.

Untitled

1

Don't be upset,
I'm still
a sapling
in your heart's courtyard.

...

4

One of these evenings,
I ought to travel with myself.

...

9

The only way for me
to find my lost memories
is to be somewhere where I can fly.

10

The wings stolen
during the Anfal assault
stayed in the desert.

11

I am looking for legs made out of wind
so that
I can get home sooner.

12

I saw the sun
going down by a pond
wearing a T-shirt with a rainbow.

1

This time,

from the other side of the ocean,

it's me and my luck,

long forgotten and left behind,

that frequent the alleyways of my childhood.

The revolution,

buried under the rocks now,

stopped dreaming a long time ago.

It allowed itself to become a prisoner of fate.

I returned to the east

in order to sit by the fireplace of wisdom.

I knew I had no one left in the cities.

I knew it was too late to look for a home.

I knew there were no heavenly gardens anymore.

It was in a meadow

where birds cannot live

that I realized reciting poetry was now impossible.

Repairs were of no use:

the bridges connecting heaven and hell had to be rebuilt entirely.

I had this really funny brother,

who put the moon in my imagination,

who reminded me of my favourite garden,

and took me to the alleyways of our childhood.

I used to wake him up early

so that he could see sunrise.

I always shared my food with him,

took him out for evening walks,

told him about the city and its history.

I gave him every plot of land I owned.

But one day,

while we were watching the birds in our courtyard,

he said he wanted to learn how to make cages.

Ever since,

the two of us had been fighting;

and it was our fights that sent me to exile.

2

I crossed the high seas—

seas that, like me, had no country,

but, unlike me, they knew their purpose.

I waited to see if the seas would burn with me.

They didn't.

At night,

the fishermen turned their lights off;

I wasn't happy about that.

I joined those waiting for rain;

we lay down on our backs near the sea,

bored and empty-handed.

I used to be in love with the sky,

but this time the sky seemed to be lost.

Instead of rain came the warplanes.

My daughter Niga asked,

"Dad, does this mean we can't go shopping?"

3

From now on,

we sit in the sun

and let our beards turn grey,

while we become strangers

to mother, death, and sea.

Here they say

God died a long time ago.

Over there,

before everyone else,

we grew wheat

and played music.

4

I am a stranger;

I come from far, far away;

I ran away from war.

Sea: I want you to be my lifelong companion.

I want the two of us to burn together.

Here,

I see no roads to take me home.

Sea: I know you are powerful;

I know also you have no time for hope.

Sea: I have been waiting for the sun to rise;

but I am just wasting my time:

the sun keeps ignoring my boat.

But then after all these years,

I am still looking forward to the day

when I can relax in the sun.

5

Sea: that evening,

when I arrived at the shore,

I saw no fishermen.

That night,

as I lay my head on a rock,

I felt disappointed

and frightened.

6

Sea: I must admit,

this time around the trip was different.

The roads were very scary;

I had no idea where I was heading.

But I could tell

you were not as burned with grief

as I was.

You also seemed to be a natural when it came to travelling.

At one point,

I travelled back in time to Sktan.

I waited for darkness to depart from the sea;

I was hoping,

but again in vain,

to get my stolen art back.

I needed to be in the sun very badly;

spring, once again, proved to be a disappointment.

And you pushed deeper and deeper into the west.

I got myself an apartment facing the east.

I had my keys,

but then by year's end

war broke out again.

The wounded died of thirst;

sanity swore never to come back.

Once again,

a mirror broke in my hand.

I remembered what my mother had said,

"My son, stay where you are;

displacement will be hard on you."

But, exile, I couldn't resist your offer;

"Freedom," you said, "was everything."

7

During the war,

time and nature,

as well as ways of death,

changed.

Well, my brother,

I had to save myself from the war.

Was that wrong?

It wasn't too long ago,

dear brother,

when poets owned the earth and the sky,

and gardens didn't lie to them.

But now poets are in retreat.

Words don't want to go near them;

they won't survive without coffee.

Brother,

life has become too hard:

luck is in hiding

and I can't stop the rain

from seeping through my roof.

Brother,

when I arrived in exile,

my luck refused to get out from its hiding place.

I spent my first night by the sea.

That night,

the wind returned wings to butterflies;

the orchards were full of kisses.

One again,

I had to rely on the kindness of words.

8

Dear brother,

isn't it about time we put our guns away?

Isn't it about time we stopped fighting under the moon?

Isn't it about time we stopped hurting our land?

My brother,

I know full well what's going on:

the peace that the morning brings

by evening is forgotten.

My brother,

I fled the war rather than fight against you.

9

Dear brother,

before I left for exile,

I was still in love with Hawler at night.

Remember my mother didn't want to see me pack?

But I am here now,

and I am coming to you, Oh Sea, for help:

help me find my way in this new world.

My brother,

I remember the time you robbed me of my little rubber ball.

I let your anger win.

It's easy to play a game;

it's even easier to ruin it.

No
Warmth

1985

His tomb is in the west.
The storm has reduced visibility to zero;
the roads cannot be seen.
The snow is too much for people to bear.
Everywhere is dark;
a strong wind is needed to break up the gloom.
His tomb is in the west.
People can be seen here and there,
running away from loneliness,
frightened,
trying to withdraw into their burrows.
It will be a long time before they reappear.

History has made you worry too much,
but when will history be thinking of you?
Your back is crooked;
no one wants to notice you.
Your heart is as generous as before,
but it doesn't get excited anymore.
History has made you worry too much.
These days,
you and history walk elbow to elbow
in the same direction:
that of the known and the unknown.
The two of you reach a child playing with water—
it's only then you begin to understand
that memory is the problem.

My Heart and Water

If my heart could be turned into a rock,
I would throw it into the water.
By getting used to water,
my heart would make the crossing a lot easier.

A hand came, secretly;
it tied me up in the cold;
then tied me up in the heat.
It made no difference:
my soul continued shouting at the world.

The End of Conflicts

The gull
was determined to keep its turf.
A crow came
and sat on a rock;
the two became a pair.
The gull raised its chicks;
the crow began crowing.
A pigeon flew out of its nest,
and sat on the same rock.
The place became known
as the triangle of birds,
or where conflicts end.

No need to build a fire;

snow won't be falling.

Put your hand inside the meadow,

and it will soon take root.

People like it that way;

the birds like it that way.

The two worlds were far apart:

one was fragmented,

the other in ruin,

but they can be made whole.

Even death cannot satisfy the storm.
Summer is over,
but its body has yet to be buried.
Empty village,
what are you waiting for?
Empty heart,
what are you waiting for?
No one will be using the roads anymore;
they've all turned yellow.
Only human connection
can save us from loneliness.

At long last
I saw water at work:
Cleverly making its way,
letting everything bathe in it.
But water has its limitations too:
it cannot return to its source.

Before Leaving

Before leaving,
he put a flower on his lapel;
his legs, however, were shaking.
An eagle flew towards his head
and landed on top.
There was nothing he could do to make the bird fly away.

It was the most depressing time:
The shadows were wrapping themselves around the earth;
fear was falling down with the rain.
Fear accompanied me to the door.
Farewell was like a dead hand:
too many questions,
too few answers.

Before exile,
I was where all the winds gathered;
I didn't have to hide from them.
On the contrary,
they were like good friends to me,
always trying not to let depression come near me.
But here,
no matter what I do,
the wind refuses to welcome me.

I made it through another autumn.
They said, "Winter uses the cold to hold onto earth."
Winter protested:
"After all the rain and the wind,
I turned once again into a humble creek,
giving nourishment to earth."
They said, "When summer comes,
you will be blown away like straw."
But that didn't happen.

Burial

We need to dig another grave;
the one we dug hit the rocks.
But we cannot dig in the dark;
besides, the cemetery is full.
Another cemetery is an option,
but his grave must be among other graves.
That's what the moon said
before granting permission for his burial.

A lonely flower
growing by a spring
wrapped itself in its petals year round.
I waited for a sweet-talker to arrive
to rescue her from loneliness.

The Shrine

It's too cold for the birds to fly;
the place is shrouded in fog.
Don't go down any further,
you'll get lost.
But it's a quiet place—
if you stay here long enough,
you'll become a shrine.

A flock of crows are waiting:
for what?
The blood of air and earth?
To receive my memoir?
It's not mine anymore.
The rain has scattered my dreams;
they're beyond recognition now.
I waited for fate.
It came.
We bonded,
we danced,
but soon it disappeared.
I have no memoir to share.

After the Storm

The storm,
having destroyed one street,
is now turning its wrath against another.
You, and your collection of bloody wounds,
where do you want to go?
The storm has tied your hands and legs.
Since you cannot move,
history and I will come to pay you a visit—
maybe we can solve your problems.

He went inside
and turned all the lights on.
He put on his best clothes.
"Come and catch me," he said.
He had just gotten out of the hospital;
memories had soured his mood;
he had thrown away his medicine.
He said,
"I'll buy a horse and a greyhound
and return to the village—
that's where I want to spend the rest of my life."
It was eight o'clock in the evening;
a severe pain invaded his bones;
he got up,
went outside,
and fell to the ground:
life left him like a liquid.
We sat by his body all night,
crying.
By early morning,
he was buried.
Soon after, his soul returned to us as a butterfly.

The Anthem of Departure

A shadow eclipsed the moon.
A pair of dogs,
left behind,
were playing joyfully.
If you are not dead already,
you soon will be,
so what would you want as your shroud?
The brightness of the moon?
Or dry grass?
Or snow high up the mountain peaks?
You try to stay behind locked doors
and move away from the colder regions.
But no matter where you are,
you'll still hear the anthem of departure.
The wolves come down in packs,
singing goodbyes.
The moon separates itself from nature;
the snow tries to achieve immortality
by keeping to itself.
So one more time:
What would you want as your shroud?

The
Evening
Snow
Dance

1979

A View

When you turn into a gentle rain,
I will follow you.
When you turn into a brook,
I will become the evergreen grass along your banks.

You used to come at night
and add more logs to the fire,
start telling me stories from long ago,
from faraway lands.
They were great stories.
I loved no one as I loved you.
Since then,
I see more wrinkles on my face,
my hair is greyer.
You stopped writing.
And even though you exist only in a painting,
I can never forget you.

That Evening

The forest avoided looking at the sky,
for that evening
it had seen too many dead bodies.
I waited and waited
but no stars appeared.

His dead body is where pollen comes to gather
and wait for the wind.
This is also where flowers from around the world come to sing,
and where lovers come to cry.

1

In the ice water of your eyes,
summer is a dry tree.
Flocks of night birds fly
from town to town
and village to village.
Your heart is a cloud
inside my heart;
it doesn't like where it is.
Your depression won't go away
until you forget me and yourself,
or until you turn my poetry into tobacco.
If you die,
die like a stream—
let people see how you were.

2

A deserted road,
a poet,
a suitcase—
nothing can describe sadness better.

3

Under a sunshine that comes and goes
my days in exile
turn into dry twigs.
Let the village girls collect them
for their evening fire.
And you—
every now and then,
you appear from under the snow,
or when the sun is out—
but you never linger.

Take the lantern
and put it by the tombstone of that grave.
In the spring
pollen
and in the summer
dry grass
will come here to dance.
The poor will be glad to see the lantern—
it will make tears look like stars.

No Return

You died in the evening;
the path to the water hole was blocked;
the link between my heart and millions of sparrows snapped.
My heart didn't know what to do;
it couldn't turn into a mountain,
for my heart and mountains stopped co-existing long ago.

Year round the snowstorm is busy doing its work;

even the wind cannot plough the snow off the mountain slopes;

no tree is in sight;

the land is bare.

Legend says:

"Once upon a time,

a traveller,

looking for honey,

slipped down a mountain slope,

head first.

His body was never found."

Returning

Late at night,
when the dogs start barking,
I say you'll return
but only to leave soon.
Please come back
before the rain sweeps away the only remaining bridge—
I would lose my mind seeing you stranded.
Until the dogs stop barking
and the stream turns calm again,
I'll have no rest.

I love you more than ever before.
Take me for what I am.
Where do you want to go?
Please don't go—
you don't know where this narrow path takes you.
Let us give our love a chance;
at least wait until autumn.
Please don't go—
please don't be tempted by the snow
to trap the little black birds.
But if you really have to go,
then you will have to put an end to my agony.

Always Anxious

It's a full moon,
but one side of the mountain
has yet to see proof of that.
That's how love is:
It's always anxious.

We were two peaks in a dense fog,
but we could always see the stars.
The moon liked us;
the sun flooded us with sunshine;
darkness flattened the hills and valleys dividing us—
that's why the mountain peaks don't understand
why we broke up.

The Shade

I have to wait until tomorrow
to enjoy the afternoon shade
created by the ancient citadel.
By early evening,
the shade covers half of the city.
It then gently disappears into darkness.
The lantern is my sole companion,
but I will let you have it.
I know you'll protect it from the rain.

Behind the mountain,
the dogs bark non-stop.
There's nothing the mountain can do,
except keep a low profile.

To Love

1

Before it gets dark,
let me see you again—
Seeing you is what keeps me alive.
I don't want to be inside;
even when it's cold,
I prefer the streets.
I know the wind will take away my winter coat;
I know one night the cold will kill me.
When you find out,
you'll sleep in peace.
You don't want
to end up in the street like me,
harassed by flies and the wind.
To love is to go crazy.

2

I promise I'll see you again.
I promise I'll hide you again.
I promise I'll take you again
to all our favourite places.
I know even the mountains cannot get in our way.
When you say, "I'm on fire,"
I promise not to call for help.

3

I know
one day you'll join the trees,
helping birds and travellers.
I know
you will then turn into a pond—
a meeting place for doves, ducks, and house martins.

4

Why do you want to go inside?
The stars have yet to appear.
Please don't go inside:
I feel weak,
I resemble a hollow tree
battered by the wind.

A Visit

Come and visit my grave,
but come only at night
and alone,
bring some flowers
and build a little fire.
"What are you doing?
Crying?
What for?
Look at me:
Now neither the storms nor the waves can cause me harm."

1

You're a vast desert
with only the shadow of the clouds visiting you
and only for a few hours a day—
and only in winter.
Your colour is grey;
you haven't seen any trees,
nor snow;
if it snows just once,
all of your sins will be forgiven,
and you'll acquire a more lively colour,
attracting all sorts of birds.

2

I remember,
you'd come to my place
sometimes in the snow,
your body shivering
as you dusted the snow off your clothes;
you always made sure my place was warm enough.
On the misty window pane,
you'd write,
"The world is nothing without love;
loving you keeps me alive."
The snow would stop,
the birds would come out again,
but you'd still be there,
standing,
looking at me—
we felt like two birds,
with no need for fire or overcoats.

The Evening Snow Dance

That evening,
I saw you off in heavy snow;
we couldn't tell spring was already upon us.
When apart,
we're like night owls.
Next time we embrace
it will be among the dandelions.
The drought comes
the rain comes
the snow comes:
the rain and the earth thank one another
after they become friends with our love.

An ancient woodland in a valley,
where flocks of sparrows gather,
where a shepherd can still be seen
sitting on a rock playing his flute,
and where daffodils greet every visitor:
I greet them back;
I greet the sparrows too.

The Fish Eagle

Before the evening is over,
the fish eagle makes its last dive,
ever careful to keep most of its body dry.
As it tries to land on a tree,
unintentionally,
it scares many birds away.

I sleep near your heart.
Please don't say,
"My heart is full of poisonous snakes."
Please don't cry for me:
Your tears will scare the earth away.
When the wind stops blowing,
we'll be better off than flowers.

That Tree

I returned to that tree,
the one on which you wrote,
"I love you forever."
I embraced it,
didn't mind the cold,
the wind,
the darkness.
When the storm became severe,
the footpath you built above the stream
helped me escape.

Your heart has been trapped in a fortress—
your leadership is drunk by night;
it's in tears by day.
Don't expect any rescue mission.

Any Time You Come

1

The storm destroyed his grave,
washing away the bones and the stones.
I still don't want you to cry;
calm will always return.

2

A bird is flying low
right above the cemetery.
Come inside my love;
my soul will warm you up.
Not being with you
is like being stuck in a deep valley.
Anytime you come,
you'll find the door of my heart wide open.

This is the body of a poet
being returned to his source:
a tree that has kept spring in the shade for many years.
But wait: is this really a body,
or a cloud,
or a forest?
A lot of birds are in the procession;
so is the snow.
Who's going to keep watch over the body tonight?
It's a beautiful night:
all the stars are out
and fear is gone.
Tomorrow
he'll be buried
among the other immortals.

The Kindness of Trees

In a rugged valley,
the road said:
"I have never seen any light above my head;
my heart cannot feel what's above—
I miss being with the trees."

A stork said:
"I won't allow old age to stop me.
I'll continue coming early every spring.
I'll go back to the same nest,
but each time I'll add fresh straw."

The road said:
"Could it be that light is even more fragile than me?
Or could it be that I am not affectionate enough?
I have no other wish,
but for light to reach my heart,
just once."

If you leave me,
we'll be as far apart as the earth and the sun:
you'll be on one side of the mountain;
I'll be on the other.
Worse, your memories will stop moving me.

A Layer of Dust

A tornado you were:
You didn't settle anywhere;
you never left the evening sky alone;
you were always tense and unpredictable.
What you've left behind
is nothing but a layer of dust.

Even if the world turns upside down,

I won't stop loving you.

What are you doing in this desert?

Moonlight won't allow your words to reach me.

That's why I must stand atop the world's ruin

and sing your name

in summer and autumn,

in winter and spring,

as the snow slowly gives way to new life

and new flowers.

No matter how things turn out between us,

your fingerprints will continue to nourish my body.

New
Poems

2012–

Where Am I?

Fourteen years in this country,
in the same neighbourhood,
and I still don't know where I belong.
With my next door neighbour on the right,
I have yet to exchange a word;
with my other neighbour, I do talk,
but no more than three times a year.
If it's summer and the sun is out,
we say, "It's a nice day."
If it's winter,
while shovelling the snow,
we say: "It's snow again."
And then just before the year is over,
he leaving,
I returning,
we exchange a few more words.

The Berlin Wall,
long the face of the Cold War,
fell in 1989,
ending the city's ideological divide:
churchgoers,
mail carriers,
freed political prisoners,
exiles—
they all celebrated together.
In East Germany,
books on communism and its promised utopia
were shoved aside;
now books on capitalism and spirituality were in demand.
The Berlin Wall came down:
the markets became free
and the secret police became a thing of the past.
But what next?
After seventy years of the Cold War,
it's hard to tell what the future will be like.
Every year,
some Germans gather where the wall once stood,
drink champagne.
Other Germans stay away,
quietly reading and reflecting in their homes.
Twenty years ago the wall came down:
I wonder, what became of all the weapons left from the Cold War?
Perhaps some ended up in Tora Bora,
fighting the West's new enemy.
The Berlin Wall is gone,
but other walls remain:
some are intended to prevent school children from being blown away;
some keep Mexicans from crossing into the US.

Walls, walls, walls:
in 1996,
near the village of Perar,
the Kurds,
divided by politics,
built their own wall.
That wall is also no more.
But I miss the thick mud walls of our old house.
I always felt safe behind them.

The times we were together,

There were no forks in the road

That took us to the place we were from.

The mountain was our neighbour

And we climbed to its top.

From there, the only world we knew

Was that which reached the view.

The times we were together,

Starlings did not delay the good tidings of spring

To our room.

The times we were together,

Technology hadn't changed our relationships:

Counting corruption money

Didn't take up our time.

We had time to love,

Time for friendship,

Time to mourn the dead.

The times we were together,

We were not voters for hire;

We still had dignity.

Most important, God had become irrelevant.

The times we were together,

Our thoughts were like sunshine.

I know we cannot change the past.

We can't jump toward the future either.

Maybe these are strange things to say

In a world calling itself postmodern.

The times we were together,

Our mother tongue was not small enough to fit in a pocket,

Eye contact was still the language of love.

The days we were together

Love had actually made us one.

The days we were together,
Even birds welcomed us.
The times we were together,
A child, inside, was leading us,
The mind and the heart were one.
But still we were in a hurry to grow up.
We came in the same boat—
You chose terror,
I became a poet.

ANFAL is the name given to Saddam Hussein's genocidal chemical attack on Kurdistan, in which 180,000 Kurdish civilians died. The name of the campaign is derived from the title of the eighth Sura of the Quran, and means "the spoils of war."

AWAGIRD is a mountain in Iraqi Kurdistan.

HALABJA is a medium-sized city in Iraqi Kurdistan that Saddam Hussein attacked with chemical weapons in 1988.

HAWLER (or ERBIL) is the sprawling capital of the Kurdistan Regional Government in northern Iraq.

KALACHI YASSEEN AGHA is a town in Iraqi Kurdistan, half an hour's drive from Erbil.

KOORAN PARK was one of Erbil's two city parks that have been swallowed up by economic development.

KOYA is a medium-sized city in Iraqi Kurdistan, an hour's drive from Erbil.

OLS is a working-class district in Ankara, the Turkish capital.

OMAR KHAWAR and his infant son lying dead following a chemical attack in 1988 has become one of the most recognizable symbols of Saddam Hussein's campaign against the Iraqi Kurds.

SKTAN is a small village in Iraqi Kurdistan where the poet got his first job as a schoolteacher.

SHARAZOUR is a fertile valley in Iraqi Kurdistan that was chemically attacked by Saddam Hussein in 1988.

SULEIMANIYA is one of Southern Kurdistan's major cities.

Acknowledgements

MANY THANKS to the University of Alberta Press—Linda Cameron for publishing my book; Peter Midgley for his great work; Alan Brownoff for his amazing design; and Cathie Crooks and Monika Igali for being a wonderful marketing team. My admiration, too, for Sharon Wilson, who does the administration work. Thank you also to Sabah Salih, my translator, Professor of English at Bloomsburg University in Pennsylvania. I would also like thank my wife Saba, my daughters Eawar and Niga, and my son Jwamer for their support.

Other Titles from The University of Alberta Press

The Man in Blue Pyjamas

A Prison Memoir

JALAL BARZANJI

SABAH A. SALIH, *Translator*

JOHN RALSTON SAUL, *Foreword*

978-0-88864-536-4 | $24.95 (T) paper

978-0-88864-611-8 | $19.99 (T) EPUB

978-0-88864-526-5 | $19.99 (T) Kindle

978-0-88864-784-9 | $19.99 (T) PDF

288 pages | 34 B&W photographs, translator's preface, foreword, map

Wayfarer Series

Memoir/Human Rights/Kurdistan

small things left behind

ELLA ZELTSERMAN

978-1-77212-002-8 | $19.95 (T) paper

978-1-77212-012-7 | $15.99 (T) EPUB

978-1-77212-013-4 | $15.99 (T) Kindle

978-1-77212-014-1 | $15.99 (T) PDF

128 pages

Robert Kroetsch Series

Poetry/Canadian Literature/Immigration

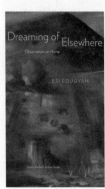

Dreaming of Elsewhere

Observations on Home

ESI EDUGYAN

MARINA ENDICOTT, *Introduction*

978-0-88864-821-1 | $10.95 (T) paper

978-0-88864-836-5 | $8.99 (T) EPUB

978-0-88864-837-2 | $8.99 (T) Kindle

978-0-88864-838-9 | $8.99 (T) PDF

56 pages | Introduction, liminaire/foreword

Copublished by Canadian Literature Centre/ Centre de littérature canadienne

Henry Kreisel Memorial Lecture Series

Canadian Literature/Essay